TH[E ...]
OF ST THÉRÈSE
OF LISIEUX
IN HER OWN WORDS

All booklets are published
thanks to the generosity of the supporters
of the Catholic Truth Society

Contents

Preface 3

Understanding Thérèse 4

Secret of Sanctity 5

Spiritual Childhood 9

Simplicity 21

The Night of the Soul 29

Charity 32

Some Prayers of St Thérèse 40

May she teach everyone "the little royal road" of the spirit of childhood, which is the exact opposite of behaving childishly, of taking no initiative and of remaining sunk in misery! We invite all men of goodwill, particularly the humble and the humiliated, to meditate on this hopeful paradox.[1]

(Pope Paul VI)

All rights reserved. First published 1932 by The Incorporated Catholic Truth Society. This edition published 2019 by The Incorporated Catholic Truth Society, 40-46 Harleyford Road, London SE11 5AY Tel: 020 7640 0042 Fax: 020 7640 0046. Copyright © 2009 The Incorporated Catholic Truth Society.

ISBN 978 1 86082 580 4

Preface

Saint Thérèse on being asked shortly before her death what was the 'Little Way' she was so eager to teach others, replied:

'It is the way of spiritual childhood, the way of trust and absolute surrender. I want to point out to souls the means that I have always found so completely successful, to tell them there is only one thing to do here below - to offer Our Lord the flowers of little sacrifices and win him by our caresses. That is how I have won him, and that is why I shall be made so welcome.'

The following extracts have been taken from the English translation of the Saint's autobiography.[2] They include in the Saint's own words, advice which she gave by letter and by counsel to those who sought her guidance.

It is hoped that the extracts may serve as sign-posts on the Little Way for those who wish to follow it.

Understanding Thérèse

We desire earnestly that all the faithful of Christ should render themselves worthy of partaking in the abundant profusion of graces resulting from the intercession of "little Thérèse". But we desire much more earnestly that all the faithful should study her in order to copy her becoming children themselves, since otherwise they cannot, according to the oracle of the Master, arrive at the Kingdom of Heaven.

If the way of spiritual childhood became general, who does not see how easily would be realised the reformation of human society... We, therefore, adopt as our own the prayer of the new Saint Thérèse with which she ends her invaluable autobiography: "O Jesus, We beseech thee to cast thy glance upon the vast number of little souls, and to choose in this world a legion of little victims worthy of thy love." Amen.'[3]

(Pope Pius XI)

Secret of Sanctity

Jesus!... O! I would so love him! Love him as he has never yet been loved.

Way of perfection

You ask me for a method of attaining perfection. I know of Love - and Love only! Our hearts are made for it alone. Sometimes I endeavour to find some other word for love; but in a land of exile words which have a beginning and an end are quite unable to render adequately the emotions of the soul, and so we must keep to the one simple word - Love.

Way of love

How sweet is the Way of Love! True, one may fall and be unfaithful to grace, but Love knows how to draw profit from everything, and quickly consumes whatever may be displeasing to Our Lord, leaving in the heart only a deep and humble peace.

But how shall I show my love, since love proves itself by deeds? I, the little one, will strew flowers, perfuming the Divine Throne with their fragrance.

I will sing Love's canticle in silvery tones. Thus will my short life be spent in thy sight, O my Beloved! To strew flowers is the only means of proving my love, and these flowers will be each word and look, each little daily sacrifice. I wish to make profit out of the smallest actions and do them all for Love. For Love's sake I wish to suffer and to rejoice: so shall I strew my flowers. Not one that I see but, singing all the while, I will scatter its petals before thee. Should my roses be gathered from amid thorns, I will sing notwithstanding, and the longer and sharper the thorns, the sweeter will grow my song.

There is but one thing to be done here below: to love Jesus, and to save souls for him that he may be more loved. We must not let slip the smallest opportunity of giving him joy. We must refuse him nothing. He is in such need of love.

Disinterested love

I do not desire the thrill of love which I can feel; if Jesus feels its thrill, then that is enough for me. It is so sweet to love him, to make him loved.

It would not disturb me if (supposing the impossible) God himself did not see my good actions. I love him so much, that I would like to give him joy without his knowing who gave it. When he does know, he is, as it were, obliged to make a return.

Offer to God the sacrifice of never gathering any fruit off your tree. If it be his will that throughout your whole life you should feel a repugnance to suffering and humiliation - if he permits all the flowers of your desires and of your goodwill to fall to the ground without any fruit appearing, do not worry. At the hour of death, in the twinkling of an eye, he will cause rich fruits to ripen on the tree of your soul.

...It is for us to console Our Lord, and not for him to be always consoling us. His heart is so tender that if you cry he will dry your tears; but thereafter he will go away sad, since you did not suffer him to repose tranquilly within you. Our Lord loves the glad of heart, the children that greet him with a smile. When will you learn to hide your troubles from him, or to tell him gaily that you are happy to suffer for him?

Thérèse at the age of 15.

Spiritual Childhood

Whosoever is a little one, let him come to me.
(*Pr* 9.4)

Self-surrender

Jesus deigns to point out to me the only way which leads to Love's divine furnace, and that way is self-surrender: it is the confidence of the little child who sleeps without fear in its father's arms. Through the mouth of Solomon, the Holy Spirit has said: 'Whosoever is a little one, let him come unto me,' and elsewhere the same Spirit of Love declares that 'to him that is little, mercy is granted.'[4] In his name, too, the Prophet Isaiah reveals how on the last day the Lord 'shall feed his flock like a shepherd: he shall gather together the lambs with his arm, and shall take them up into his bosom.'[5]

And, as though all these proofs were insufficient, the same Prophet, whose inspired gaze penetrated the depths of eternity, cried out: 'Thus saith the Lord: You shall be carried at the breasts and upon the knees they shall caress you. As one whom the mother caresseth, so will I comfort you.'[6]

If all weak and imperfect souls such as mine felt as I do, none would despair of reaching the summit of the mountain of Love, since Jesus does not look for deeds, but only for gratitude and self-surrender.

Now I have no further desire unless it be to love Jesus even unto folly! Love alone draws me. I wish for neither suffering nor death, yet both are precious to me, and I have long called upon them as the messengers of joy. Already I have suffered much; already it has seemed to me that my barque was nearing the Eternal Shore. From my earliest years I believed the Little Flower would be gathered in her springtime, but now the spirit of self-abandonment is my sole guide - I have no other compass. I am no longer able to ask eagerly for anything save the perfect accomplishment of God's design on my soul.

I desire neither death nor life. Were Our Lord to offer me my choice, I would not choose. I only will what he wills, and I am pleased with whatever he does. I have no fear of the last struggle, or of any pain, however great, which my illness may bring. God has always been my help; he has led me by the hand since I was a child and I count on him now. Even though suffering should reach its furthest limits I am certain he will never forsake me.

Spiritual Childhood

Keeping little

How little known is the merciful love of the Heart of Jesus! It is true that to enjoy that treasure we must humble ourselves, must confess our nothingness... and here is where many a soul draws back.

It is possible to remain little even in the most responsible position, and besides is it not written that at the last day 'The Lord will arise and save the meek and lowly ones of the earth'?[7] He does not say 'to judge' but 'to save'!

You do wrong to find fault, and to try to make everyone see things from your point of view. We desire to be as little children. Now, little children do not know what is best. Everything is right in their eyes. Let us imitate them.

When we keep little we recognise our own nothingness and expect everything from the goodness of God, exactly as a little child expects everything from its father. Nothing worries us, not even the amassing of spiritual riches.

Again, being as a little child with God means that we do not attribute to ourselves the virtues we may possess, in the belief that we are capable of something. It implies, on the contrary, our recognition of the fact that God places the treasure of virtue in the hand of his little child for him to use as he needs it, though all the while it is God's treasure.

Finally, to keep little means not to lose courage at the sight of our faults. Little children often tumble, but they are too small to suffer grievous injury.

Courage

Do not let your weakness make you unhappy. When, in the morning, we feel no courage or strength for the practice of virtue, it is really a grace: it is the time to 'lay the axe to the root of the trees',[8] relying upon Jesus alone. If we fall, an act of love will set all right, and Jesus smiles. He helps us without seeming to do so; and the tears which sinners cause him to shed are wiped away by our feeble love. Love can do all things. The most impossible tasks seem to it easy and sweet. You know well that Our Lord does not look so much at the greatness of our actions, or even at their difficulty, as at the love with which we do them. What, then, have we to fear?

Trust in God's justice

Though one must indeed be pure before appearing in the sight of the All-Holy God, still I know that he is infinitely just, and the very justice which terrifies so many souls is the source of all my confidence and joy. Justice is not only stern severity towards the guilty; it takes account of the good intention, and gives to virtue its reward. Indeed, I hope as much from the justice of God as from his mercy. 'He is compassionate and merciful, long-suffering and plenteous in mercy. For he knoweth our frame, he remembereth that we are dust. As a father hath compassion on his children, so hath the Lord compassion on them that fear him.'[9]

Love of the Sacred Heart

If the greatest sinner on earth should repent at the moment of death, and draw his last breath in an act of love, neither the many graces he had abused, nor the many sins he had committed, would stand in his way. Our Lord would see nothing, count nothing, but the sinner's last prayer, and without delay he would receive him into the arms of his mercy.

But to make him thus blind and incapable of reckoning the number of our sins, we must approach him through his Heart - on that side he is defenceless.

Confidence

With daring confidence, and reckless of self, I will remain there till death, my gaze fixed upon the Divine Sun. Nothing shall affright me, neither wind nor rain; and should impenetrable clouds conceal from my eyes the Orb of Love, should it seem to me that beyond this life there is darkness only, this would be the hour of perfect joy, the hour in which to urge my confidence to its uttermost bounds, for knowing that beyond the dark clouds my Sun is still shining, I should never dare to change my place... O Divine Sun, I am happy to feel myself so small and frail in thy presence, and my heart is at peace.

We can never have too much confidence in our God who is so mighty and so merciful. As we hope in him so shall we receive.

The Heart of Jesus is more grieved by the thousand little imperfections of his friends than by the faults, even grave, which his enemies commit. But his heart thrills with joy when he has to deal with all those who truly love, and who after each little fault come to fling themselves into his arms, imploring forgiveness.

Patience with ourselves

It may be that at some future day my present state will appear to me full of defects, but nothing now surprises me. Nor does my utter helplessness distress me; I even glory in it, and expect each day to reveal some fresh imperfection. Indeed these lights on my own nothingness do me more good than lights on matters of faith.

Spiritual Childhood

The remembrance of my faults humbles me, and helps me never to rely upon my own strength, which is mere weakness. More than all, it speaks to me of mercy and of love. When a soul with childlike trust casts her faults into Love's all-devouring furnace, how can they escape being utterly consumed?

I know that many saints have passed their lives in the practice of amazing penance for the sake of expiating their sins. But what of that? 'In my Father's house there are many mansions.'[10] These are the words of Jesus, and therefore I follow the path he marks out for me; I try to be nowise concerned about myself, and to abandon unreservedly to him the work he deigns to accomplish in my soul.

He reaches out his hand to us, the very moment he sees us fully convinced of our nothingness, and hears us cry out: 'My foot stumbles, Lord, but thy mercy is my strength.'[11] Should we attempt great things, however, even under pretext of zeal, he deserts us. So all we have to do is to humble ourselves, to bear with meekness our imperfections. Herein lies - for us - true holiness.

Do not think we can find love without suffering, for our nature remains and must be taken into account; but suffering puts great treasures within our reach. Indeed it is our very livelihood and so precious that Jesus came down upon earth on purpose to possess it. Of course, we should like to suffer generously and nobly; we should like never to fall. What an illusion! What does it matter if I fall at every moment! In that way I realise my weakness, and the gain is considerable. My God, thou seest how little I am good for, away from thy divine arms; and if thou leavest me alone, well, it is because it pleases thee to see me lie on the ground. Then why should I be troubled?

If you are willing to bear in peace the trial of not being pleased with yourself, you will be offering the Divine Master a home in your heart. It is true that you will suffer, because you will be like a stranger to your own house; but do not be afraid - the poorer you are, the more Jesus will love you. I know that he is better pleased to see you stumbling in the night upon a stony road, than walking in the full light of day upon a path carpeted with flowers, because these flowers might delay your advance.

Prayer

For me, prayer is an uplifting of the heart, a glance towards Heaven, a cry of gratitude and of love in times of sorrow as well as of joy. It is something noble, something supernatural, which expands the soul and unites it to God.

To secure a hearing there is no need to recite set prayers composed for the occasion... I have not the courage to search through books for beautiful prayers; they are so numerous, that it would only make my head ache, and besides, each one is more lovely than the other. Unable either to say them all or to choose between them, I do as a child would do who cannot read - I say just what I want to say to God, quite simply and he never fails to understand.

Apostolate of prayer

Why does he deign to say: 'Pray ye the Lord of the harvest that he send forth labourers'?[12] It is because the delicacy of his love for us surpasses all understanding, that he wishes us to share in all he does. The Creator of the universe awaits the prayer of a poor little soul to save a multitude of other souls, ransomed, like her, at the price of his blood.

Our vocation is not to go forth and reap in our Father's fields. Jesus does not say to us: 'Look down and reap the harvest.' Our mission is even more sublime. 'Lift up your eyes and see,'[13] he tells us. 'See how in Heaven there are empty thrones. It is for you to fill them... You are as Moses praying on the mountain so ask me for labourers and they shall be sent. I only await a prayer, a sigh!'

Is not the apostleship of prayer - so to speak - higher than that of the spoken word? It is for us by prayer to train workers who will spread the glad tidings of the Gospel and who will save countless souls - the souls to whom we shall be the spiritual mothers. What then have we to envy in the priests of the Lord?

Holy Communion

I suppose I ought to he distressed that I so often fall asleep during meditation and thanksgiving after Holy Communion, but I reflect that little children, asleep or awake, are equally dear to their parents; that to perform operations doctors put their patients to sleep; and finally, that 'The Lord knoweth our frame. He remembereth that we are but dust.'[14]

There is no time when I have less consolation - yet this is not to be wondered at, since it is not for my own satisfaction that I desire to receive Our Lord but solely to give him pleasure.

Picturing my soul as a piece of waste ground, I beg of Our Lady to take away my imperfections, which are as heaps of rubbish, and to raise upon it a spacious pavilion worthy of Heaven, and beautify it with her own adornments. I next invite thither all the Angels and Saints to sing canticles of love, and it seems to me that Jesus is well pleased to find himself welcomed with such magnificence, while I, too, share his joy. But this does not keep off distractions and drowsiness, and I often resolve to continue my thanksgiving throughout the day in amends for having made it so badly in choir.

You see, dear Mother, that my way is not the way of fear; I can always find means to be happy and to profit by my failings, and Our Lord himself encourages me to do so.

Dryness in prayer

When my state of spiritual aridity is such that not a single good thought will come, I repeat very slowly, the 'Our Father' and the 'Hail Mary', which suffice to console me, and provide divine food for my soul.

When I am in this state of spiritual dryness, unable to pray, or to practise virtue, I look for little opportunities, for the smallest trifles, to give pleasure to Jesus: a smile or a kind word, for instance, when I would wish to be silent, or to show that I am bored. If no such occasion offer, I try at least to say over and over again that I love him. This is not heard, and it keeps alive the fire in my heart. Even should the fire of love seem dead, I would still throw my tiny straws on the ashes, and I am confident it would light up again.

It is true I am not always faithful, but I never lose courage. I leave myself in the arms of Our Lord. He teaches me 'to draw profit from everything, from the good and from the bad which he finds in me'.[15] He teaches me to speculate in the bank of love, or rather it is he who speculates for me, without telling me how he does it - that is his affair, not mine. I have but to surrender myself wholly to him, to do so without reserve, without even the satisfaction of knowing what it is all bringing to me... For I am not the prodigal child, and Jesus need not trouble about a feast for me - I am always with him.[16]

Simplicity

Their loss is gain who all forsake
To find thy love, O Jesu mine!
For thee my ointment jar I break,
The perfume of my life is thine.

Praying for others

The days would be too short to ask in detail for the needs of each soul and I am afraid I might forget something important. Complicated methods are not for simple souls and, as I am one of these, Our Lord himself has inspired me with a very simple way of fulfilling my obligations.

One day, after Holy Communion, he made me understand these words of Solomon: 'Draw me: we will run after thee to the odour of thy ointments.'[17] O my Jesus, there is no need then to say: In drawing me, draw also the souls that I love. The words 'Draw me' suffice. When a soul has been captivated by the odour of thy perfumes she cannot run alone; as a natural consequence of her attraction towards thee, all those whom she loves are drawn in her train.

In asking to be drawn, we seek an intimate union with the object that has led our heart captive. If iron and fire were endowed with reason, and the iron could say, 'Draw me!' would this not prove its wish to be identified with the fire to the point of sharing its substance? Well, such is precisely my prayer. I ask Jesus to draw me into the fire of his Love, and to unite me so closely to himself that he may live and act in me. I feel that the more the fire of love consumes my heart, the more frequently shall I cry, 'Draw me!' and the more also will those souls who come in contact with me run swiftly in the sweet odour of the Beloved.

Distractions

As soon as I am aware of them, I pray for those people the thought of whom is diverting my attention, and in this way they reap benefits from my distractions... I accept all for the love of God, even the wildest fancies that cross my mind.

Mortification

Far from resembling those heroic souls who from their childhood use fast and scourge and chain to discipline the flesh, I made my mortifications consist simply in checking my self-will, keeping back an impatient answer, rendering a small service in a quiet way, and a hundred other similar things.

Simplicity

I have a longing for those heart-wounds, those pin-pricks which inflict so much pain. I know of no ecstasy to which I do not prefer sacrifice. There I find happiness, and there alone. The slender reed has no fear of being broken, for it is planted beside the waters of Love. When, therefore, it bends before the gale, it gathers strength in the refreshing stream, and longs for yet another storm to pass and sway its head. My very weakness makes me strong. No harm can come to me, since in whatever happens I see only the tender hand of Jesus... Besides, no suffering is too big a price to pay for the glorious palm.

I endeavoured above all to practise little hidden acts of virtue, such as folding the mantles which the Sisters had forgotten and being on the altar to render them help. I had also a great attraction towards penance, although I was not allowed to satisfy the desire. Indeed the only mortification I was permitted was the overcoming of my self-love, which did me far more good than any bodily penance could have done.

God does not despise these hidden struggles with ourselves, so much richer in merit because they are unseen: 'The patient man is better than the valiant, and he that ruleth his spirit than he that taketh cities.'[18] Through our little acts of charity, practised in the dark, as it were, we obtain the conversion of the heathen, help the missionaries, and gain for them plentiful alms, thus building both spiritual and material dwellings for our Eucharistic God.

Hidden sacrifices

For a long time my place at meditation was near a Sister who fidgeted incessantly, either with her rosary or with something else. Possibly I alone heard her because of my very sensitive ear, but I cannot tell you to what an extent I was tried by the irritating noise. There was a strong temptation to turn round and with one glance to silence the offender; yet in my heart I knew I ought to bear with her patiently, for the love of God first of all, and also to avoid causing her pain. I therefore remained quiet, but the effort cost me so much that sometimes I was bathed in perspiration, and my meditation consisted merely in the prayer of suffering. Finally, I sought a way of gaining peace, in my inmost heart at least, and so I tried to find pleasure in the disagreeable noise. Instead of trying not to hear it, I set myself to listen attentively as though it were delightful music, and my meditation - which was not the prayer of quiet - was passed in offering this music to Our Lord.

On another occasion when I was engaged in the laundry, the Sister opposite to me, who was washing handkerchiefs, kept splashing me continually with dirty water. My first impulse was to draw back and wipe my face in order to show that I wanted her to be more careful. The next moment, however, I saw the folly of refusing treasures thus generously offered, and I carefully refrained from betraying any annoyance. On the contrary I made such efforts to welcome the shower of dirty water that at the end of half an hour I had taken quite a fancy to the novel kind of aspersion, and resolved to return as often as possible to the place where such precious treasures were freely bestowed.

Offering little joys

It seems to me that if our sacrifices take Jesus captive, our joys make him prisoner too. All that is needed to attain this is that, instead of giving ourselves over to selfish happiness, we offer to our Spouse the little joys he scatters in our path to charm our hearts and draw them towards him.

Idle fears

You have grieved me greatly by abstaining from Holy Communion, because you have grieved Our Lord. The devil must be very cunning to deceive a soul in this way... The treacherous creature knows quite well that when a soul is striving to belong wholly to God he cannot cause her to sin, so he merely tries to persuade her that she falls. This is a considerable gain, but not enough to satisfy his hatred, so he aims at something more, and tries to shut out Jesus from a tabernacle which Jesus covets. Unable to enter the sanctuary himself, he wishes that at least it remain empty and without its God. Alas! what will become of that poor little heart? When the devil has succeeded in keeping a soul from Holy Communion he has gained all his ends... while Jesus weeps!...

Remember that our sweet Jesus is there in the Tabernacle expressly for you and you alone. Remember that he burns with the desire to enter your heart. Do not listen to the enemy. Laugh him to scorn, and go without fear to receive Jesus, the God of peace and of love...

I assure you I have found that this is the only means of ridding oneself of the devil. When he sees he is losing his time, he leaves us in peace.

In truth, it is impossible that a heart which can find rest only in contemplation of the Tabernacle - and yours is such, you tell me - could so far offend Our Lord as not to be able to receive him... What does offend Jesus, what wounds him to the heart, is want of confidence.

Pray that the best portion of your life may not be overshadowed by idle fears. We have only life's brief

Simplicity

moments to spend for the glory of God, and well does Satan know it. That is why he employs every ruse to make us consume them in useless labour. Dear sister, go often to Holy Communion, go very often - that is your one remedy.

The Little Way

St Thérèse of Lisieux.

The Night of the Soul

It is so sweet to serve God in the dark night and in the midst of trial. After all we have but this life in which to live by faith.

Walking in darkness

I give thanks to Jesus for making me walk in darkness, and in the darkness I enjoy profound peace. Indeed, I consent to remain through all my religious life in the gloomy passage into which he has led me. I desire only that my darkness may obtain light for sinners. I am content, nay, full of joy, to be without all consolation. I should be ashamed if my love were like that of earthly brides who are ever looking for gifts from their bridegrooms, or seeking to catch the smile which fills them with delight.

Thérèse, the little Spouse of Jesus, loves him for himself.

Desolation

When my heart, weary of the enveloping darkness, tries to find some rest and strength in the thought of an everlasting life to come, my anguish only increases. It seems to me that the darkness itself, borrowing the voice of the unbeliever, cries mockingly: 'You dream of a land of light and fragrance, you believe that the Creator of these wonders will be for ever yours, you think to escape one day from the mists in which you now languish. Hope on!... Hope on!... Look forward to death! It will give you, not what you hope for, but a night darker still, the night of utter nothingness!

Perseverance in faith

I have made more acts of faith during the past year than in all the rest of my life. Whenever my enemy provokes me to combat, I try to behave like a gallant soldier. Aware that a duel is an act of cowardice, I turn my back on the foe without once looking him in the face; then hastening to my Saviour I tell him that I am ready to shed my blood as a witness to my belief in Heaven. I tell him that if he will deign to open it for eternity to poor unbelievers, I am content to sacrifice during my life all joyous thoughts of the Home that awaits me.

Joy of suffering

And so in spite of this trial which robs me all sense of enjoyment, I can still say: 'Thou hast given me, O Lord, a delight in thy doings.'[19] For is there a greater joy than to suffer for thy love, O my

The Night of the Soul

God? The more intense and more hidden the suffering the more dost thou value it. And even if by an impossibility thou shouldst not be aware of my affliction, I should be still happy to bear it, in the hope that by my tears I might prevent or atone for one sin against faith.

You may think that I am exaggerating the night of my soul. If one judged by the poems I have composed this year it might seem that I have been inundated with consolation, that I am a child for whom the veil of Faith is almost rent asunder... But it is not a veil.., it is a wall which reaches to the very heavens, shutting out the starry sky.

... And yet I have never experienced more fully the sweetness and mercy of Our Lord. He did not send this heavy cross when it would, I believe, have discouraged me, but chose a time when I was able to bear it. Now it does no more than deprive me of all natural satisfaction in my longing for Heaven.

It seems to me that nothing stands in the way of my going thither. I have no longer any great desires, beyond that of loving till I die of love.

Charity

Be zealous for the better gifts. And I show unto you a yet more excellent way. (1 *Co* 12:3)

Vocation of love

Charity gave me the key to my vocation. I understood that since the Church is a body composed of different members, she could not lack the most necessary and most nobly endowed of all the bodily organs. I understood, therefore, that the Church has a heart - and a heart on fire with love. I saw, too, that love alone imparts life to all the members, so that should love ever fail, apostles would no longer preach the Gospel and martyrs would refuse to shed their blood. Finally, I realised that love includes every vocation, that love is all things, that love is eternal, reaching down through the ages and stretching to the uttermost limits of earth.

Beside myself with joy, I cried out: 'O Jesus, my Love, my vocation is found at last - my vocation is love!' I have found my place in the bosom of the Church, and this place, O My God, thou hast thyself given to me: in the heart of the Church; my Mother, I will be Love!... Thus shall I be all things and my dream will be fulfilled.

Loving our neighbour

Greater love than this no man hath, that a man lay down his life for his friends.[20] As I meditated on these divine words, I understood how imperfect was the love I bore my Sisters in religion, and that I did not love them as Our Lord does. Now I know that true charity consists in bearing all my neighbour's defects, in not being surprised at mistakes, but in being edified at the smallest virtues.

... Should the devil bring before me the defects of a Sister, I hasten to look for her virtues and good motives. I call to mind that though I may have seen her fall once, she may have gained many victories over herself which in her humility she conceals, and also that what appears to be a fault may very well, owing to the good intention that prompted it, be an act of virtue.

... From all this I conclude that I ought to seek the companionship of those Sisters for whom I feel a natural aversion, and try to be their good Samaritan. It frequently needs only a word or a smile to impart fresh life to a despondent soul. Yet it is not merely in the hope of bringing consolation that I wish to be kind; if it were, I should soon be discouraged, for often well-intentioned words are totally misunderstood. Consequently, in order that I may lose neither time nor labour, I try to act solely to please Our Lord.

Give generously

'If any man take away thy coat, let go thy cloak also unto him.'[21]

It seems to me that to give up one's cloak is to renounce every right, and look upon oneself as the servant, the slave of all. Divested of a cloak, however, it is easier to walk or run, so the Master adds:

'And whosoever will force thee one mile, go with him other two.'[22] Hence it is not enough for me to give to the one who asks, I ought to anticipate the wish; I should show myself honoured by the request for service, and if anything set apart for my use be taken away I should appear glad to be rid of it.

'For him that would borrow of thee turn not away.'[23] Neither should I be kind for the sake of being considered so, nor in the hope that the Sister will return the service, for once again it is written: 'If you lend to them of whom you hope to receive, what thanks are to you? For sinners also lend to sinners for to receive as much. But you, do good and lend, hoping for nothing thereby, and your reward shall be great.'[24]

Along this path it is but the first step that costs - even on earth the reward will be great.

O my Jesus! Thou dost never ask what is impossible; thou knowest better than I how frail and imperfect I am; thou knowest that I shall never love my Sisters as thou hast loved them, unless thou lovest them thyself within me, my dearest Master. It is because thou dost desire to grant me this grace, that thou has given a new Commandment, and dearly do I cherish it, since it proves to me that it is thy Will to love in me all those thou dost bid me love.

Give us souls

I would spread the Gospel in all parts of the earth, even to the farthest isles. I would be a missionary, but not for a few years only. Were it possible, I should wish to have been one from the world's creation and to remain one till the end of time.

Give to us souls, dear Lord... We thirst for souls - above all, for the souls of apostles and martyrs... that through them we may inflame all poor sinners with love of thee.

The end cannot be reached without adopting the means, and since Our Lord had made me understand that it was through the cross he would give me souls, the more crosses I encountered the stronger became my attraction to suffering.

I am convinced that no remedies have the power to cure me, but I have made a covenant with God that they may be for the benefit of poor missionaries who have neither time nor means to take care of themselves.

(During an illness the Saint had been advised to take a short walk in the garden each day for a quarter of an hour. Seeing how this exhausted her, one of the Sisters urged her not to take it as it only tired her. 'That is true,' she answered, 'but do you know what gives me strength? I offer each step for some missionary, thinking that, somewhere far away, one of them is worn out by his apostolic labours, and to lessen his fatigue I offer mine to God.')

Love is repaid

While thinking one day of those who offer themselves as victims to the Justice of God, and who turn aside the punishment due to sinners, taking it upon themselves, I felt such an offering to be both noble and generous. I was very far, nevertheless, from feeling myself drawn to make it, and from the depths of my heart I cried: 'O my Divine Master, shall thy Justice alone find atoning victims? Has not thy Merciful Love need of them also?

On every side it is ignored and rejected... those hearts on which thou wouldst lavish it turn to creatures and seek their happiness in the miserable satisfaction of a moment, rather than cast themselves into thy arms - into the ecstatic fires of thy infinite Love.[25]

O my God, must that Love which is disdained lie hidden in thy Heart? It seems to me that if thou shouldst find souls offering themselves as a holocaust to thy Love, thou wouldst consume them rapidly and wouldst be pleased to set free those flames of infinite tenderness now imprisoned in thy Heart. If thy Justice which avenges itself upon earth must needs be satisfied, how much more must thy Merciful Love desire to inflame souls, since 'Thy Mercy reacheth even to the Heavens'![26] O Jesus, permit that I may be that happy victim - consume thy holocaust with the fire of Divine Love!

I am but a weak and helpless child, but my very weakness makes me dare to offer myself, O Jesus, as victim...

... Forgive me, O Jesus, if I tell thee that thy Love reacheth even unto madness, and at the sight of such folly what wilt thou but that my own heart should leap up to thee? How could my trust know any bounds?

I know well that for thy sake the Saints have made themselves foolish - being 'eagles' they have done great things. Too little for such mighty deeds, my folly lies in the hope that thy Love accepts me as a victim, and in my confidence that the Angels and Saints will help me to fly unto thee with thy own wings, O my Divine Eagle! As long as thou willest I shall remain with my gaze fixed upon thee, for I long to be fascinated by thy divine eyes, I long to become

Love's prey. I am filled with the hope that one day thou wilt swoop down upon me, and bearing me away to the source of all Love, wilt plunge me at last into its glowing abyss, that I may become for ever its happy victim.

Call to little souls

Why fear to offer yourself as a victim to God's Merciful Love? If it were to his Divine Justice you might have reason to fear, but the Merciful Love will have pity on your weakness and will treat you with tenderest mercy.

You who love Jesus and long to be his little victim, do you not understand that the more weak and wretched we are, the better material do we make for his consuming and transfiguring fire?... The simple desire to be a victim suffices, but we must also consent to remain always poor and helpless, and here lies the difficulty: 'Where shall we find one that is truly poor in spirit? We must seek him afar off,' says the author of the Imitation.[27] He does not say that we must search among great souls, but 'afar off' - that is to say, in abasement and in nothingness. Let us remain far from all that dazzles, loving our littleness, and content to have no joy. Then we shall be truly poor in spirit, and Jesus will come to seek us, however far off we may be, and transform us into flames of love...

O Jesus! would that I could tell all little souls of thy ineffable condescension! If by any possibility thou couldst find one weaker than mine, one which should abandon itself with perfect trust to thy Infinite Mercy, I feel that thou wouldst take delight in loading that soul with still greater favours. But whence these desires, O my Spouse, to make known the secrets of... thy Love? Is it not thou alone who hast taught them to me and canst thou not likewise reveal them to others? I know that thou canst and I beseech thee to do so...

I beseech thee to cast thy glance upon a vast number of little souls: I entreat thee to choose in this world a legion of little victims worthy of thy love.

Some Prayers of St Thérèse

Act of oblation

O my God, O Most Blessed Trinity, I desire to love thee and to make thee loved - to labour for the glory of thy Church by saving souls here upon earth and by delivering those suffering in Purgatory. I desire to fulfil perfectly thy will, and to reach the degree of glory thou hast prepared for me in thy kingdom. In a word, I wish to be holy, but, knowing how helpless I am, I beseech thee, my God, to be thyself my holiness.

Since thou hast loved me so much as to give me thy Only-Begotten Son to be my Saviour and my Spouse, the infinite treasures of his merits are mine. I offer them gladly to thee, and I beg to thee to look on me through the eyes of Jesus, and in his Heart aflame with love. Moreover, I offer thee all the merits of the Saints in Heaven and on earth, together with their acts of love, and those of the holy Angels. Lastly, I offer thee, O Blessed Trinity, the love and the merits of the Blessed Virgin, my dearest Mother - to her I commit this oblation, praying her to present it to thee.

During the days of his life on earth her divine Son, my sweet Spouse, spoke these words: 'If you ask the Father anything in my Name, he will give it you.'[28] Therefore I am certain thou wilt grant my prayer. O my God, I know that the more thou wishest to bestow, the more thou dost make us desire. In my heart I feel boundless desires, and I confidently beseech thee to take possession of my soul. I cannot receive thee in Holy Communion as often as I should wish; but art thou not all-powerful? Abide in me as thou dost in the tabernacle - never abandon thy little victim. I long to console thee for ungrateful sinners, and I implore thee to take from me all liberty to cause thee displeasure. If through weakness I should chance to fall, may a glance from thine eyes straightway cleanse my soul, and consume all my imperfections - as fire transforms all things into itself.

I thank thee, O my God, for all the graces thou hast granted me, especially for having purified me in the crucible of suffering. At the day of judgment I shall gaze with joy upon thee, carrying thy sceptre of the cross. And since thou hast deigned to give me this previous cross as my portion, I hope to be like unto thee in Paradise, and to behold the sacred wounds of thy Passion shine on my glorified body.

After earth's exile I hope to possess thee eternally, but I do not seek to lay up treasures in heaven. I wish to labour for thy love alone - with the sole aim of pleasing thee, of consoling thy Sacred Heart, and of saving souls who will love thee through eternity.

When the evening of life comes, I shall stand before thee with empty hands, because I do not ask thee, my God, to take account of my works. All our good deeds are blemished in thine eyes. I wish therefore to be robed with thine own justice, and to receive from thy love the everlasting gift of thyself. I desire no other throne but thee, O my Beloved!

In thy sight time is naught - 'one day is a thousand years'.[29] Thou canst in a single instant prepare me to appear before thee.

In order that my life may be one act of perfect love, I offer myself as a holocaust to thy Merciful Love, imploring thee to consume me unceasingly and to allow the floods of infinite tenderness gathered up in thee to overflow into my soul, that so I may become a martyr of thy love, O my God! May this martyrdom one day release me from my earthly prison, after having prepared me to appear before thee, and may my soul take its flight - without delay - into the eternal embrace of thy merciful Love!

O my Beloved, I desire at every beat of my heart to renew this oblation an infinite number of times, 'till the shadows retire'[30] and everlastingly I can tell thee my love face to face.[31]

Prayer to the Holy Child

O little Jesus, my only treasure, I abandon myself to every one of thine adorable whims. I seek no other joy than that of making thee smile. Grant me the graces and the virtues of thy holy childhood, so that on the day of my birth into Heaven the angels and saints may recognise in thy little spouse... Thérèse of the Child Jesus.

Prayer to the Holy Face

O adorable Face of Jesus, sole beauty which ravisheth my heart, vouchsafe to impress on my soul thy divine likeness, so that it may not be possible for thee to look at thy spouse without beholding thyself. O my Beloved, for love of thee I am content not to see here on earth the sweetness of thy glance, nor to feel the ineffable kiss of thy sacred lips, but I beg of thee to inflame me with thy love, so that it may consume me quickly, and that soon Thérèse of the Holy Face may behold thy glorious countenance in Heaven.

Prayer for humility

I implore thee, dear Jesus, to send me a humiliation whensoever I try to set myself above others. Thou knowest my weakness. Each morning I resolve to be humble, and in the evening I recognise that I have often been guilty of pride. The sight of these faults tempts me to discouragement; yet I know that discouragement is itself but a form of pride. I wish therefore, O my God, to build all my trust upon thee. As thou canst do all things, deign to implant in my soul this virtue which I desire, and to obtain it from thy infinite mercy I will often say to thee: 'Jesus, meek and humble of heart, make my heart like unto thine.'[32]

Morning offering

O my God! I offer thee all my actions of this day for the intentions and for the glory of the Sacred Heart of Jesus. I desire to sanctify every beat of my heart, my every thought, my simplest works, by uniting them to its infinite merits; and I wish to make reparation for my sins by casting them into the furnace of its merciful love.

O my God! I ask of thee for myself and for those whom I hold dear the grace to fulfil perfectly thy holy will, to accept for love of thee the joys and sorrows of this passing life, so that we may one day be united together in Heaven for all eternity. Amen.[33]

Prayer to the Little Flower

O Saint Thérèse of the Child Jesus, who during thy short life on earth became a mirror of angelic purity, of love strong as death, and of whole-hearted abandonment to God, now that thou rejoicest in the reward of thy virtues cast a glance of pity on me as I leave all things in thy hands. Make my troubles thine own - speak a word for me to Our Lady Immaculate, whose flower of special love thou wert - to that Queen of Heaven 'who smiled on thee at the dawn of life'. Beg her as Queen of the Heart of Jesus to obtain for me by her powerful intercession the grace I yearn for so ardently at this moment, and that she join with it a blessing that may strengthen me during life, defend me at the hour of death, and lead me straight on to a happy eternity. Amen.[34]

Prayer

O God, who didst inflame with thy spirit of love the soul of St Thérèse of the Child Jesus, grant that we also may love thee, and may make thee much loved. Amen.

Endnotes

[1] Letter of Pope Paul VI to the Bishop of Bayeux and Lisieux, 2nd January, 1973.
[2] By kind permission of Father T. N. Taylor.
[3] Sermon of Pope Pius XI at Canonisation of Saint Thérèse, 17th May, 1925.
[4] *Ws* 6.7.
[5] *Is* 40.11
[6] *Is* 66, 12, 23.
[7] Cf. *Ps* 75.10.
[8] *Mt* 3.10.
[9] *Ps* 102.8, 13, 14.
[10] *Jn* 14.2.
[11] *Ps* 93.18.
[12] *Mt* 9.38.
[13] *Jn* 4.35.
[14] *Ps* 102.14.
[15] St John of the Cross.
[16] Cf. *Lk* 15.31.
[17] *Sg* 1.3.
[18] *Pr* 16.32.
[19] *Ps* 91.5.
[20] *Jn* 15.23.
[21] *Mt* 5.40.
[22] *Mt* 5.41.
[23] *Mt* 5.42.
[24] *Lk* 6.34, 35.
[25] Motto of St Thérèse of Lisieux, from St John of the Cross.
[26] Cf. *Ps* 35.6.
[27] Cf. Imit II, ch 9.4.
[28] *Jn* 16.23.
[29] *Ps* 39.4.
[30] *Sg* 4.6.
[31] This Prayer was found after the death of Saint Thérèse in the copy of the Gospels which she carried night and day close to her heart.
[32] Extract from prayer for Humility written for a Novice.
[33] The original manuscript is preserved at Carfin.
[34] From the Novena to Saint Thérèse.

Thérèse - Teacher of Prayer

St Thérèse of Lisieux has much to teach us about prayer. This delightfully simple booklet will help all those wishing to follow the young Carmelite's way of praying with the heart. In doing so, Brother Craig takes us through some of the richest traditions: Eucharistic adoration, devotion to Our Lady and veneration of the saints and angels. Above all we are reminded by Thomas a Kempis that 'Grace walks in simplicity, in doing all things purely for God'. This is what Thérèse can teach us. Prayers to and by Therese are included.

ISBN: 978 1 86082 480 7

CTS Code: D693

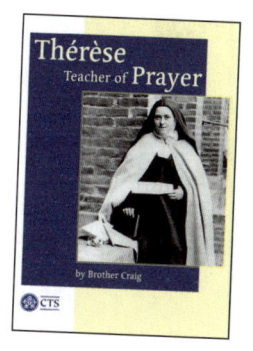

Has this book helped you?
Spread the word!

@CTSpublishers

/CTSpublishers

ctscatholiccompass.org

Let us know!
marketing@ctsbooks.org
+44 (0)207 640 0042

Learn, love, live your faith.
www.CTSbooks.org